ACCEPTANCE, RESPECT, AND APPRECIATION OF DIFFERENCE

XINA M. UHL

PowerKiDS
press™

T0026783

Published in 2023 by The Rosen Publishing Group, Inc.
2544 Clinton Street, Buffalo, NY 14224

First Edition

Editor: Greg Roza
Book Design: Michael Flynn

Photo Credits: Cover Ground Picture/Shutterstock.com; (series background) tavizta/Shutterstock.com; p. 5 CarlosBarquero/Shutterstock.com; p. 6 Vitalii Vodolazskyi/Shutterstock.com; p. 7 Darren Baker/Shutterstock.com; p. 9 tilialucida/Shutterstock.com; p. 11 (Buzz Aldrin) courtesy of NASA; p. 11 (Franz Kafka) https://commons.wikimedia.org/wiki/File:Franz_Kafka,_1923.jpg; pp. 13, 25 Monkey Business Images/Shutterstock.com; p. 14 CREATISTA/Shutterstock.com; p. 15 Johnny Silvercloud/Shutterstock.com; p. 17 Motortion Films/Shutterstock.com; p. 18 Cecil Bo Dzwowa/Shutterstock.com; p. 19 Ruchuda Boonplien/Shutterstock.com; p. 21 Lightfield Studios/Shutterstock.com; p. 22 Dmitry Demidovich/Shutterstock.com; p. 23 AlessandroBiascioli/Shutterstock.com; p. 26 VH-studio/Shutterstock.com; p. 27 dominika zara/Shutterstock.com; p. 29 Prostock-studio/Shutterstock.com.

Cataloging-in-Publication Data

Names: Uhl, Xina M.
Title: Acceptance, respect, and appreciation of difference / Xina M. Uhl.
Description: New York : Powerkids Press, 2023. | Series: Spotlight on a fair and equal society | Includes glossary and index.
Identifiers: ISBN 9781538387900 (pbk.) | ISBN 9781538387931 (library bound) | ISBN 9781538387948 (ebook)
Subjects: LCSH: Cultural pluralism--Juvenile literature. | Multiculturalism--Juvenile literature. | Toleration--Juvenile literature.
Classification: LCC HM1271.U45 2023 | DDC 305.8--dc23

Manufactured in the United States of America

Some of the images in this book illustrate individuals who are models. The depictions do not imply actual situations or events.

CPSIA Compliance Information: Batch #CWPK23. For further information contact Rosen Publishing at 1-800-237-9932.

CONTENTS

CHAPTER ONE

WHAT IS BEING OPEN-MINDED?

Being open-minded means making a good-faith effort to understand people who are different from you. You have an open mind when you are willing to listen and learn about other people's beliefs and practices. Reflecting on how you think about differences can be a test of open-mindedness. If you can consider different beliefs, ideas, and values with an accepting attitude, you can help people get along even if they are different.

For people to get along, they must respect each other and their differences. Being open-minded means willingness to seek common ground and overcome **bias** and **intolerance**. Acceptance doesn't always mean you agree with others. It does mean that you recognize a person's right to differ from you and still be treated with respect.

Differences can be celebrated, accepted, and respected.

CHAPTER TWO

BIAS AND THE BRAIN

Many people would probably say that they are open-minded and not **prejudiced**. However, anyone can be biased, even if they're not fully aware of it. You can have negative, or harmful and unwanted, attitudes toward a group or a person without completely realizing it. These attitudes are learned and can be unlearned.

If you think you aren't biased, think again. Check in with your judgments and attitudes. Interrupt your thoughts and take a second look at your reactions.

Sometimes you might judge another person or make a decision because of a **stereotype**. People tend to put other people in different groups based on visible (or other) features. This may come from the way the brain looks for patterns. There are reasons that happens. However, making overly general judgments about a group or person's social identity can lead to more bias and unfair beliefs and actions.

CHAPTER THREE

CHECKING IN ON BELIEFS AND ATTITUDES

Human brains receive information almost 300 times faster than they can process it. So, sometimes they bundle up some details into broad beliefs and attitudes that may be untrue. Here are some examples.

Many people have lumped together their beliefs about dogs into one viewpoint. They may see only the good or only the bad. Even though all dogs are not the same, some people may react as if they are always dangerous or always friendly. Neither way of thinking is based on reality.

Similarly, some may do the same thing with people. Many educators may encourage girls to study and focus on science and math, and many women excel at, or do very well in, science and engineering careers. However, some people still have false beliefs and attitudes that girls aren't good at science or math. Because of this, these people may direct girls toward other fields.

It can be hard to admit that we have biases, but doing so can lead to more opportunities for all people.

CHAPTER FOUR

WHAT IS THE OPPOSITE OF OPEN-MINDED?

Of course, the opposite of open is closed. Just like doors or windows, minds can be closed instead of open. That makes sense if you think about how some people resist new ideas or reject different beliefs and values because they don't match their own. People with closed-minded thinking may hold onto the familiar and may not consider or accept other possibilities. Even listening to and understanding someone else's perspective, values, or view of the world can be very hard for closed-minded people.

There are times when people avoid those who are different from them because they have negative attitudes about them. Often these attitudes are learned and stay in place unless people open their minds to listen and learn. They may change their minds. Awareness and new perspectives, or viewpoints, may build bridges between people instead of walls.

An oft-repeated quote is "Your mind is like a parachute. It doesn't work if it's not open." It's been attributed, or credited, to writer Franz Kafka, rock-and-roll legend Frank Zappa, and astronaut Edwin "Buzz" Aldrin.

EDWIN "BUZZ" ALDRIN

FRANZ KAFKA

CHAPTER FIVE

BUILDING BRIDGES

Kids just like you can find ways to bring people together and take down walls that divide **diverse** neighborhoods and communities. Eating lunch with a student who always sits alone in the cafeteria may help take down a wall of **isolation**. Getting to know a person who has been left out can build a bridge of kindness and **empathy**.

In one case, a school with students from many parts of the world decided to create a new way to connect people. It offered opportunities for kids from different countries, who speak different languages and have different cultures, to get together and talk. These gatherings were called Multicultural Meets. A diverse panel of people would invite kids to ask them questions about their beliefs, culture, experiences, or interests. Just starting this conversation changed attitudes and beliefs that could have divided communities. Those who took part developed new friendships.

Learning about a person who is different from you can open your mind to new knowledge, customs, and more.

CHAPTER SIX

REMOVING WALLS, OPENING MINDS

In some areas of the world, people with different beliefs live in communities divided by physical walls. The walls may separate groups of people with a strong history of conflict. This has been the case in South Africa, Northern Ireland, and Palestine. These situations are often many centuries old. Sometimes this long-held hatred breaks out into violence and even war.

Starting in 1969, people built "Peace Walls" in Belfast, Northern Ireland, to separate communities of Catholics and Protestants. Many of the walls are famous for their political murals. In 2012, the authorities of Northern Ireland started to remove the Peace Walls.

Close-minded people continue to build walls between groups. These divisions may have to do with poverty, **ethnicity**, race, culture, or religion. During the COVID-19 **pandemic**, for example, some people expressed distrust and even hatred for Asian Americans. These people wrongly believed that the pandemic started because of aspects of Chinese culture.

Both kinds of walls can be torn down, however. Communities can become whole again if people learn to open their minds.

CHAPTER SEVEN

RACISM AND RESPONSIBILITY

Racism is the belief that certain races are superior to others. It's based on beliefs that are learned from others, and it leads to negative attitudes and actions. With the goal of fairness and **equity**, young people can recognize racial bias in themselves and others and take on the responsibility to stand up against racism.

Personal responsibility to stand up for what's right can be a big challenge, but even one person doing the right thing pushes back against racism. If you have empathy for people who are mistreated because of racism, you know the importance of speaking up. Speaking with courage and respect can make you a valuable supporter. However, sometimes being the one to speak up can result in negative pressure from those who hold racist beliefs. Doing the right thing and taking action against bias takes courage.

It's painful when a person is excluded or **discriminated** against because of their race.

CHAPTER EIGHT

HOW TO LEARN OPEN-MINDEDNESS

Open-mindedness can be learned. Technology offers endless possibilities for students to interact with others around the world. Kids in many different countries can use computers to chat or speak live onscreen with kids in your school. People can interact with others who might dress, think, and act differently. You can learn to overcome stereotypes and **misconceptions**. You can learn more about similarities and differences and think about other ideas and ways of life.

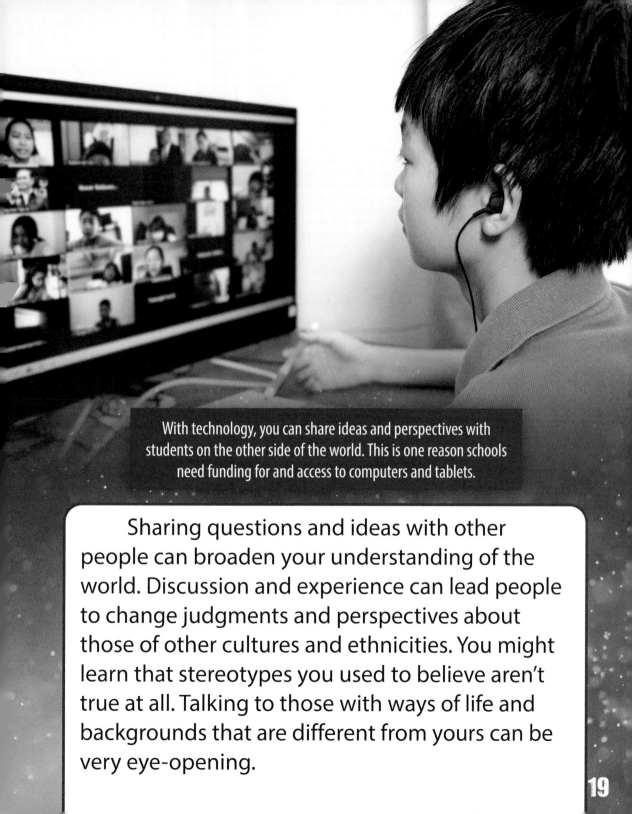

With technology, you can share ideas and perspectives with students on the other side of the world. This is one reason schools need funding for and access to computers and tablets.

Sharing questions and ideas with other people can broaden your understanding of the world. Discussion and experience can lead people to change judgments and perspectives about those of other cultures and ethnicities. You might learn that stereotypes you used to believe aren't true at all. Talking to those with ways of life and backgrounds that are different from yours can be very eye-opening.

CHAPTER NINE

CHANGE STARTS WITH HELLO

Some parts of society have made progress on issues of poverty and injustice, but they still exist. Some people also continue to focus on stereotypes and bias. Some still make judgments and decisions and hold perspectives that are biased and unfair.

The path to social justice is a path to changing minds and hearts. Vernā Myers is an expert in teaching people about **inclusion** and diversity. She defines bias as "stories we make up about people before we know who they actually are."

Opening your mind to change these views means opening up to experiences and connections with others who are different from you. This also means stepping outside the familiar and the comfortable connections you already have to meet and get to know other students, neighbors, or community members. Building that bridge can lead to trust and new understanding.

Starting change can be as simple as just saying hello or sharing lunchtime together.

CHAPTER TEN

TOLERANCE AND ACCEPTANCE

The path to equity and social justice depends on open-mindedness. However, changing the beliefs and attitudes that lead to inequity and injustice can be very challenging. Even as many people work for diversity, fairness, and justice, many others hold onto prejudice, bias, and negative judgments about others.

CHANGE STARTS IN THE MIND

Activists within the **LGBTQ+** community have worked very hard in favor of tolerance and acceptance for many years.

Sometimes, changing what people do can comes before changing what they think. There need to be **consequences** for violating people's rights. Public opinion and expectations from groups and communities can help stop hateful or unfair actions or behavior.

Tolerance and acceptance are a first step on the path to equity and social justice. Accepting diverse communities is a start. For people to peacefully exist together depends on tolerance of differences, even if many attitudes and beliefs still need to change.

CHAPTER ELEVEN

OPEN-MINDEDNESS AT WORK

Open-mindedness is not always as easy as you might think. Being open to new ideas and new experiences means that you're actively paying attention to your thoughts. Open-mindedness means you're willing to listen, consider new ideas thoughtfully, ask questions, and gather information for understanding. You're ready to use evidence to challenge your own beliefs. You're thinking about what other people are thinking. Further, you are ready to change the beliefs and attitudes that that are wrong and close-minded.

Open-minded people keep their curiosity alive and are OK having their ideas questioned by others. They work at keeping an empathetic attitude and believe that everyone is free to hold their own perspectives. Communicating about diverse perspectives opens your mind and your world. Seeing different sides of an issue takes mental effort.

Active listening is mindful listening. Thinking about what another person is saying increases empathy.

CHAPTER TWELVE

JUDGMENTS AND PERSPECTIVES

Your brain may take shortcuts when making judgments and decisions. False information taken from first impressions can be an unfair barrier to empathy or fairness. Your brain may take the easy way out and rely on false impressions about people or experiences. "Snap judgment" means making a quick judgement about someone new before you get to know them. Stereotypes and bias about groups support these mental shortcuts.

The Special Olympics, founded in 1968, alllow people with disabilities to show off their athletic talents.

For example, encountering someone who is different can trigger shortcuts in your thinking. It can be easy to make unfair judgments. Someone with a disability may be a talented athlete. A person who has trouble in school may have a learning difference. Stereotypes about many types of people might be wrong.

Getting to know the whole story about a person and who they truly are is important. Everyone in this world is different and has different strengths and talents.

CHAPTER THIRTEEN

PROBLEM SOLVING

If you and your peers witness problems that result from unfair judgments, attitudes, and actions, you have a challenge to deal with. Bullies may isolate, insult, and harm others and use their power in person and online. Some people may have negative attitudes about others based on meaningless differences. These attitudes can cause many problems and much hurt.

Working together, you can be agents of positive change and learn how to solve problems. Start with identifying the problem you want to solve and setting a goal. Working with others, investigate available allies who can help you accomplish this goal, including teachers or counselors who can help you identify possible solutions. Plan your steps to take action and gather the resources you will need. Put your plan into action and watch to see if it works. Use what you learn to refine further action.

Active citizens can solve problems and help the world become more fair and equal.

CHAPTER FOURTEEN

CHECKLIST FOR AN OPEN MIND

You are in charge of your attitudes, judgments, and perspectives. You can work for positive change by being open-minded and respectful. The following checklist can help you reach your goals.

- Respect for others is an important first step when working for acceptance and tolerance.
- Tolerance leads to coexistence and helps remove negative attitudes.
- Acceptance opens the door to shared communication and experience.
- Respect opens the door to fairness and equity.
- Reflecting on your beliefs and attitudes is a way to help yourself be open-minded.
- You are in charge of your own beliefs and ideas as you grow and change.
- Seeing or hearing bias is a challenge for positive action or words.
- Push yourself out of your comfort zone to meet and understand others.
- Be curious and work on your knowledge and understanding of other kinds of people.
- Make a promise to make this world a better place for everyone!

GLOSSARY

bias (BYE-uhs) A tendency to believe that some ideas, people, etc., are better than others.

consequence (KAHN-suh-kwens) Something produced by something or following from a condition.

discriminate (dih-SKRIH-muh-nayt) To treat people unequally based on class, race, or religion.

diverse (duh-VUHRS) Having many different types, forms, or ideas.

empathy (EHM-puh-thee) Being aware of and sharing someone else's feelings.

ethnicity (eth-NIH-suh-tee) A particular cultural group.

equity (EH-kwuh-tee) Freedom from bias or favoritism.

inclusion (in-CLOO-shun) The act of including people in a group or community.

intolerance (ihn-TAH-luh-rens) A reluctance to grant rights to other people.

isolation (i-suh-LAY-shun) The state of being kept apart from others.

LGBTQ+ (el gee bee tee kyu PLUS) An abbreviation for "lesbian, gay, bisexual, transgender, queer or questioning." The "+" stands for others not represented by these letters.

misconception (mihs-kun-SEP-shun) A wrong or inaccurate idea.

pandemic (pan-DEH-mihk) An outbreak of a disease that occurs over a wide geographic area and typically affects a significant proportion of the population

prejudiced (PREH-juh-duhst) Having an unfair feeling of dislike for a person or group because of race or other differences.

stereotype (STAYR-ee-oh-typ) A commonly held idea about a group of people that isn't necessarily true.

INDEX

PRIMARY SOURCE LIST

Page 11
Astronaut Edwin "Buzz" Aldrin. Photograph. October 18, 1963. Johnson Space Center, Houston, Texas. Held by NASA.

Page 11
Franz Kafka. Photograph. 1923–1924. From Franz Kafka Museum, Prague, Czech Republic.

Page 14
Walls dividing Catholic neighborhoods from Protestant neighborhoods. Photograph. August 1, 2018. Belfast, Northern Ireland.

TITLES IN THIS SERIES

PowerKiDS
press

ISBN: 9781538387900

9 781538 387900